MW01480553

POLITICALLY INCORRECT SICK JOKES

BY
JAMES BUFFINGTON

A POLITISISFUN.COM HUMOR GOURMET APPETIZER

© 2008 James H. Buffington
all rights reserved. No part of this book may be
reproduced except brief excerpts used in praise of
the author and his work.

Cover design: James H. Buffington
Clipart courtesy of Clipart.com, © 2008
Used under license.

ISBN 144040240X
EAN-13 9781440402401

"I can't come in to work today, boss. I'm sick."
"How sick are you?"
"I'm sleeping with my sister."

How many houseboys does it take to fill a swimming pool? 52, but you need a really big blender.

"If I want your advice, I'll read your entrails"

Little Willie met my sister
Wasn't long until he kissed her
He taught her so many tricks
Now he's doing 4 to 6.

A beautiful babe was walking
through the woods with her
new date, not realizing he was
a psychopath. It was a dark and
cloudy night with gaping
shadows everywhere.
"This forest really creeps me
out," she observed.
"What are you complaining
about?" asked the psycho.
"I've got to walk back alone."

Why do gays make great Christians?
They turn the other cheek.

"How many ADHD kids does it take to change a light bulb?"
"I don't know."
"Wanna ride our bikes?"

Why did Jesus not replace the rock in front of his cave on Easter Sunday?
He was born in a barn

"Mommy, can I go swimming?"
"Don't be silly. You know it would rust your hooks."

"Mommy, can I play in the sandbox?"
"Not until we find a better place to bury Daddy."

"Mommy, I hate sister's guts!"
"Shut up and eat what's in front of you."

Beans! Beans!
The musical fruit!
The more you eat
The more you toot
The more you toot
The better you feel
Beans! Beans!
For every meal

"Gosh, Dad, was that Bobby
Bonds who just hit that home
run?"
"What do you care, Willie?
You're blind!"

What do you do if you see
your mother in law staggering
across your front lawn?
Reload.

"Doctor, I still can't see!"
cried the little girl after the
operation.
"April Fool!"

What's the difference between
a mashed potato and a pussy?
A mashed potato doesn't make
it's own gravy.

Then there was the psycho
who sent his girlfriend a heart
for Valentine's Day.
Still beating……

A silly young man from Hong
   Kong
Had hands that were skinny
   and long
He ate rice with his fingers
The taste of it lingers
But now all his fingers are
   gone.

How do you get 4 little old ladies to shout "Fuck!?"
Yell "Bingo!"

"Does anyone on this plane know how to pray?"
"I do!"
"Good. You pray. We're one parachute short."

"For Christmas I got my wife a complete mink outfit. Two traps and a shotgun."

"How can you make sure a
man puts the toilet seat down?
Cut off his dick.

"How long are you in for?"
"99 years. And you?"
"75"
"You take the cot by the door.
You'll be out first."

Willie, with a thirst for gore,
Nailed the baby to the floor.
Momma said with humor
    quaint
Careful, Will, you'll mar
    the paint!

"You're at death's door," said the doctor, "but don't worry. I'll pull you through!"

"Mommy, what's a vampire?"
"Shut up and eat your soup before it clots."

"Mommy, can I brush my teeth?"
"Okay. Get them out of the jar."

"Mommy, can I have some soda pop?"
"Shut up and finish your beer."

A man gives his son twenty bucks on his 16th birthday and told him to go down to the local cathouse for his first piece. As he's on his way he runs into his granny. She asks him where he's going and he tells her. Granny tells him to save his money, takes him back to her cottage and deflowers him.

When the boy gets home Dad asks, "Well, son how was it?"

"Great! I got laid and saved the twenty bucks!"

"How did you do that?"

"I ran into granny and she took care of me for nothing!"

"What! You mean you screwed my mother?"

"Why not? You screw mine."

What did the cannibal do after he dumped his wife?
Wiped his butt.

"Understand you buried your wife last week."
"Had to. Dead, you know."

A kid walks up do his dad and asks, "Can I have $20 for a blowjob?"
"I don't know," replied dad.
"Are you any good?"

"I had to give up archery."
"Lose all your arrows?"
"Nope. They're stuck in Daddy."

Then there was the gay choir boy who choked on his first hymn.

"I finally cured my kid of biting his nails."
"How did you do that?"
"Knocked his teeth out."

"Why, Dad, why?" moaned the young man to his father.

"Why what, son?"

"I was out of town for a week! I telegraphed my girl I was going to get back a day early. I went over to her house and found her screwing some other guy! Why. Dad? Why?"

"Well, son, maybe she didn't get the telegram."

First bum: " Hey, what's wrong with your finger?"

Second bum: "I was downtown picking up some cigarettes and some guy stepped on my hand."

The doctor told the young lady, "Congratulations, you can tell your husband you're going to have a baby."

"Oh, I'm not married."

"Really? Where's the father?"

"Home watching our other two kids."

"This makes three. Why don't you two get married?"

"Oh, he's just not my type."

FAMOUS LAST WORDS
"I don't see how they make a profit on this stuff at $1.25 bottle…"

Singles Bar
A place where the girls are looking for husbands and the husbands are looking for girls.

Doctor: "I have good news and bad news for you."
Patient: "What's the good news?"
Doctor: "The good news is that your penis is going to grow 5 inches longer."
Patient: "What's the bad news?"
Doctor: "It's malignant."

"You haven't got a complex. You are inferior."

A boy walks in on his parents making love. "What are you doing, Mommy?"
Thinking quickly Mommy replied, "I'm sucking the air out of Daddy."
"But the maid just blew him up this morning!"

"No one cares if I drink myself to death."
"I do. You're using my liquor."

There's a new restaurant that prints your check on a condom. You can wine and dine her and stick her with the bill.

What has 75 balls and fucks old ladies?
Bingo.

Redneck Famous Last Words
"Hey, watch me do this!"

An elderly couple in their nineties went to see a lawyer. "We want to get a divorce," explained the husband.
"How long have you been married?"
"73 years."
"Good, Lord! Why did you wait so long?"
"We wanted to wait 'til the children died."

"How come you shot your husband with a bow and arrow?
"I didn't want to wake the children."

A high roller died and was being put to his final rest. The minister began his eulogy. "Big Ralph isn't really dead. He only sleeps…"
Came a voice from the back, "I got 5 grand says he don't wake up!"

Why are racetracks so clean?
All the horse's asses are in the stands.

"Daddy! Daddy! What's wife swapping?"
"Go next door and ask your Mother."

"I had to shoot Fido last week."
"Was he mad?"
"He wasn't too happy."

A funeral director approached the widow of the old man who was being buried. "How old are you," he asked.
"93."
"Hardly worth going home, is it?"

What's the best thing about a woman with small hands?
She makes your dick look bigger.

Then there was the cannibal who ate the missionary and got his first taste of religion.

How do you get a nun pregnant?
Dress her like an altar boy.

What do Eggs Benedict and a blowjob have in common?
You can't get either one at home.

"I'm sorry, Mrs. Lincoln. No refunds."

How do you get revenge on a blind man fucking your wife?
Shoot his guide dog.

"Mommy, sister's stuck up!"
"Why do you say that?"
"She won't come out of the refrigerator."

"Willie, why did you kick your sister in the stomach?"
"It's not my fault. She turned around too quick."

"George Bush just hanged himself!"
"Have they cut him down?"
"He's not dead yet."

What's brown and has holes in it?
Swiss shit.

"My wife and I sure had a good time at the beach this summer. First she'd bury me in the sand, then I'd bury her. Next year I'm going to go back and dig her up."

Only 2% of gays start life that way.
The rest get sucked into it.

"Knock! Knock!"
"Who's there?"
"Polish burglar."

Where do little Smurfs come from?
Smucking.

"The baby swallowed the matches!"
"Here, use my lighter."

There's a new all female delivery service called UPMS They deliver whenever the fuck they feel like and don't you dare complain!

There's a new deodorant called "Umpire." It's for guys with foul balls.

"The entire universe is rushing away at an ever faster rate."
'Here, try these breath mints."

Why did Frosty The Snowman pull his pants down?
He heard the snow blower coming.

Two rednecks are out hunting and one accidentally shoots the other. So he loads his buddy on in the pick, drives to hospital and rushes him into the emergency room. As the doctor examines the wounded redneck his buddy asks, "Well, Doc, is he gonna make it."
"He's have a better chance if you hadn't gutted him."

Two city slickers go hunting.
In a terrible accident one
shoots the other, who falls
motionless to the ground,
The first city slicker whips out
his cell phone and calls 911!
"Help!" he cries. "We're
hunting and I shot my buddy! I
think he's dead!"
"Okay," soothes the operator,
"just relax and everything will
be fine. First, let's make sure
your friend is dead…."
The operator hears a shot ring
out.
"Okay, now what?"

Why should women use
contraceptive sponges?
After fucking they can do the
dishes.

HIRE THE HANDICAPPED
They're fun to watch

Why do tampons have strings?
So you can eat and floss

A guy catches his neighbor screwing his wife. He grabs his rifle and shouts, "I'm gonna blow your balls off!"
"C'mon, give me a chance!"
"Okay, swing 'em!"

Why did God create woman?
Sheep can't cook.

Why did God create man?
Vibrators can't mow lawns.

A business man is on a trip and decides to pick up a gift for his wife. So he wanders around town and spies a watch in a store window he likes. So he goes into the store and says to the clerk," I'd like that watch in the window."

"I'm sorry, sir. That watch is not for sale."

"Not for sale? What kind of jewelry store is this?

"It's not a jewelry store. We neuter cats."

"Then why do you have a watch in the window?"

"What would you put there?"

"I want to be just like you when I grow up, Dad!"
"You mean you want to be a top salesperson?"
"No! I want to fuck Mom!"

Why is pubic hair soft and curly?
So it won't poke your eyes out.

What's the difference between a clitoris and a remote control?
A man won't stop looking for a remote.

What's invisible and smells
like rabbit?
Bunny farts.

What's so boring about
fucking a blonde?
Waiting in line.

What's red and green and goes
"Whirrrrr?"
A frog in a blender.

The traveling salesman, alone in the strange city, wandered into a local bar. The only other patron was lovely young lady, sitting by herself.

Soon they started a conversation and the salesman was amazed to learn that this girl was a rarity. She came from one of the richest families in the state. She had a PhD in psychology, had authored several books, spoke 5 languages fluently and danced like a professional.

As closing time arrived she invited him back to her apartment.

The salesman accepted and moments later they were at her place. She opened the door, the salesman entered and was shocked.

"Hey, there's a dead horse in the middle of the floor!"

"Well, I never said I was neat."

Why don't women have brains?

They don't have cocks to put them in.

Two lawyers are walking down the street when a beautiful babe walks by.

"Let's fuck her!" suggests the first.

"Out of what?"

A guy is walking along the beach and finds a bottle. When he opens it a genie flies out.

"I will grant you three wishes," promises the genie.

"Well, first, I'd like a bright red Mercedes."

Poof! The car appeared.

"Next I'd like a big mansion."

Poof! They were now in a luxurious mansion.

"Lastly, I'd like to be irresistible to women."

Poof! He became a box of chocolates.

Then there was the cheating wife who treated her lover like dirt.
She hid him under the bed.

Dogs are better than men. If a dog wants his balls licked he does it himself.

"Mommy, when I grow up will I get a husband like Daddy?"
"Certainly, you will."
"But if I don't get married will I end up like Aunt Martha?"
"I suppose so, yes."
"Damn, a girl can't win either way!"

What's the difference between a woman and a trampoline? Men take off their shoes before jumping on a trampoline.

It's an absolute waste of time spanking an 18 year old girl. But look at the fun you could have!

A doctor is walking down the street. A passerby stops him and says, "You've got a thermometer behind your ear." "Oh, crap! Some asshole's got my pen!"

A traveling salesman was going through the mountains when he felt nature call. Spying a shack ahead, he stopped and knocked on the door. A hillbilly opened the door.

'Howdy," he greeted.

"Hi," said the salesman, "I was wondering if I could use your bathroom?"

"Got a two seater right around back. Help yourself."

So the salesman went round back and opened the door. There on one of the seats was another hillbilly.

"C'mon in, Plenty of room." invited the second hillbilly.

So the salesman entered and dropped his drawers, and sat.

As he did so the hillbilly got up. As he pulled up his pants some change fell out of his pocket and down the hole. The hillbilly pulled out a twenty dollar bill and dropped that down the hole as well.
"What did you do that for?" asked the startled salesman.
"You don't think I'm going down there for thirty five cents, do you?"

Why do Canadians fuck doggie style?
So they can both watch hockey.

What's the difference between a slave and a tire?
Tires don't sing when you put the chains on.

What's the first symptom of AIDS?
A cock up your butt.

Make love Rodeo Style.
Do your wife from behind, grab her tits and say, "These are almost as good as your sisters'"

"I went fishing with my boyfriend"
"Catch anything?"
"I'll know in a few days."

How do you get your man to shout your name and gasp for breath?
Hold a pillow over his face.

Why did Bill Clinton name his dog "Buddy?"
No one at the White House wanted to shout, "Come, Spot!"

A traveling salesman was driving through the country when he felt the call of nature. He stopped by the road near a farmhouse next to a pumpkin patch. As a joke he cut off the top of a pumpkin, hollowed it out and took a dump in it.

Then he put the whole thing back together and drove off on his way.

On the return trip he came to the same field and felt a bit guilty about what he had done. So he pulled up to the farmhouse and knocked.

"Howdy," greeted the farmer who opened the door.

"Hi," returned the salesman.

"I'm afraid I did something not

very nice." And he proceeded to explain what he had done. The farmer listened and when the salesman finished he moseyed to the phone and dialed.

"Hi, Sis," he said. "You were right about that pie."

She has a clit like a pickle."
"That big?"
"That sour."

Butch visited the local cathouse for an evening of fun. The madam fixed him up with three babes in the best suite in the joint and they had a grand time.

When butch went to pay his bill the Madam said, "No charge. It's on the house."

The next week he returned and asked for the suite and the same three girls.

"That'll be a thousand dollars," replied the Madam.

"A thousand dollars! Last week it was free!"

"Last week was a pay per view webcast."

Jesus and Satan were arguing all over creation over who was better with computers.

Finally God sat them down before 2 PCs. "Okay, you have 2 hours to show me what you've got. Write programs, design websites, whatever!"

So Jesus and Satan began typing furiously away. After an hour and fifty five minutes the network crashed!

It came up 6 minutes later. Satan cried in fury! All his hard work was gone! He looked over and saw Jesus printing out his programs.

"He must have cheated!" cried Satan.

"Sorry," shrugged God. "Jesus saves."

Redneck Safe Sex
Tying the sheep's legs together
so it won't kick

Why are men like laxatives?
They irritate the crap out of
you

How can you tell a man is well
hung?
He turns blue and stops
struggling.

What does your asshole do
when you have an orgasm?
He shouts out, "Hey, what's
that buzzing in the bathroom?"

How are old people like
Slinkies?
They're both amusing when
they fall down stairs.

Have you seen Stevie
Wonders' new car?
Neither has he.

An old coot was talking to his doctor.

"So," asked the doctor, "how's your sex life?"

"Well, two weeks ago I picked up a really swell 20 year old. Then last week I bedded a hot little grad student. And this weekend I seduced a nifty young barmaid."

"All these women!" exclaimed the doctor. "I hope you're taking precautions!"

"Sure!" returned the geezer. "I give them a phony name and number!"

Cats are better than men.
When a cat sticks his butt in
your face he doesn't expect
you to lick it.

Loser
A guy who tries to get laid at a
family reunion.

"If I had some ham I could
make a ham sandwich if I had
some bread."

A construction worker comes home early and finds another guy in bed with his wife. Furious, he hits the other man over the head with a wrench and knocks him unconscious. When the man regains consciousness he finds he's naked in the garage with his cock locked in a vise. On the workbench next to him is a dull, rusty hacksaw.

"Please, mister, don't cut it off!" pleads the cheater."

"Don't worry, I won't," promises the construction worker. "I'm going to set the garage on fire."

The lawyer was uneasy. His millionaire client was up on a murder charge and things looked grim. Desperate, he secretly contacted a poor lady juror with no husband and three hungry mouths to feed. He offered her a million dollars if she could get her client found guilty of second degree manslaughter instead. She agreed.

After the trial the jury met for a nerve racking week, finally bringing in the second degree manslaughter verdict.

A couple days later the lawyer went to the lady's house with $1,000,000 cash.

"Thanks for you're hard work," said the lawyer. "How'd you do it?"
"It wasn't easy getting that verdict. Those other folk thought he was innocent."

Lawyer:, "So, Mrs. Jones, why did you clobber your husband with an ashtray?"
"The table lamp was too heavy."

A one hundred and five year old man and his ninety eight year old wife checked into their hotel room. "I think I'll lay down a bit," said the man. "Okay," said his wife, "I'm going down to play the slots." And with that she left.

Three hours later she returned and found her husband in the arms of a sexy young hooker. With a scream she picked him up and threw him out the window.

Horrified, the hooker screamed, "But we're on the twenty fifth floor!"

"At his age, if he can screw, he can fly!"

Why is it most guys can't
make the football team but any
cheerleader can?

There was a young fellow from
    France
Who loved to cum in his pants.
His mother said sadly
You're just like your Daddy
Jerking off in the dark with
    your lance.

How does a geek give head?
He interfaces with your laptop.

Why do geeks masturbate?
To get in touch with their feelings.

What do geeks call sperm on the ceiling?
A successful launch.

Why did the geek castrate himself?
He wanted to get his rocks off.

Geeks have wonderful sexual experiences. They just don't have anyone to share them with.

Why do geeks jerk off so much?
Their tongues are too short.

Why did the geek go shopping for a new ass?
His old one had a crack in it.

A beach boy who loved to
    have fun
Kept screwing his girl in the
    sun
And his ass, being bare
Baked to medium rare
While his girl was crying
    "Well done!"

What kind of orgy do Indian
spiritual leaders attend?
Guruope Sex.

If the Pilgrims shot bobcats
instead of turkeys we'd all be
eating pussy on Thanksgiving.

March is National Cat Month
Make someone's pussy happy

Hot Tub
A balling bowl

What's the difference between
men and jellybeans?
Jellybeans come in different
colors.

Three missionaries are captured by natives in darkest Africa. They were bound and tied to stakes.

The Chief approaches the first and says, "You have a choice. Ombata or death!"

"I'll take ombata!"

"Very well," says the Chief. The natives untie the missionary and all the men of the village proceed to have anal and oral sex with the poor man, then let him go.

The Chief approaches the second missionary and says, "You have a choice. Ombata or death!"

The missionary sweats for a while, then says, "Ombata."

"Very well," says the Chief. So the natives untie the man and rape him repeatedly and let him go,

The Chief approaches the third missionary. "Ombata or death?"

Defiantly, chin held high, the missionary proclaims, "I choose death!"

"Very well! Death by ombata!"

Mary had a little sheep
With the sheep she went to
    sleep
The sheep turned out to be a
    ram
Mary had a little lamb

A guy saddles up to a babe in a bar.
"Want to play magic?" he asks.
"How to we play"
"We go back to my place. We screw. You disappear."

How can you tell a California orange from a Florida orange? When you suck them, the California orange sucks back.

"Daddy, what's a drag queen?
"Shut up and unhook my bra."

"Do you know the difference between a cocksucker and a corned beef sandwich?"
"No."
"Let's do lunch."

How can you tell the linemen from the receivers at the team training table?
The receivers peel the bananas before they eat them.

Why has Haiti never won the America's Cup race?
It's hard to win with 856 people on board.

A gay goes to an Oriental massage parlor for the first time. He's shown to a room with a nice bed and a side table filled with oils and fragrances. He gets naked and lies down.

A few minutes later a lovely Oriental woman and enters and begins to give him a massage. After ten minutes she asks, "Would you like a hand job?"

"You know it!"

"I'll be right back, " she coos and glides out of the room. Fifteen minutes later she pokes her head back in. "Are you through yet?

Jesus walks into a Holiday Inn, tosses the desk clerk three nails and asks, "Can you put me up for the night?"

YANKEE
Same thing as a quickie, but you do it yourself.

Men are like trains.
They always stop before you get off.

A priest approaches the hat check girl in a ritzy hotel and asks, "Why don't you come up to my room?"

"Oh, Father, I couldn't do that!"

"It's ok. It is written in the Bible."

So she agrees and goes up to his room.

"Why don't you take off your clothes?" asks the priest."

Ooh, Father, that would be a sin!"

"It's ok," soothes the priest.

"It's written in the Bible."

So the girl removes her clothes.

"Now," says the priest, "Let's make love."

"That's in the Bible?" asks the girl.

"Certainly."

"I want to see it."

So the priest takes the Gideon bible out of the desk, opens it and reads: "The hat check girl screws."

How is a prostitute like a police station?

Dicks are always going in and out.

What does the Godfather have in common with Pete Rose.

4,000 hits.

SIGN IN MEN'S ROOM
Please do not throw cigarette
butts in the urinal
They clog and are difficult to
light when soggy.

What do football players like
better than a cold Budweiser?
A warm Busch.

FAME
What you get for dying at the
right time.

A guy walks into a bar. He notices a piano in the corner, but no one is playing it. He goes up to the bartender and asks, " Could I play a song for a drink?"

It was the regular piano player's night off, so the barkeep says, "Sure, buddy." So the guy strides over to the piano, sits down and for the next three minutes played the most beautiful song anyone in the bar had ever heard. By the time he's finished the whole room is in tears.

As he gets his drink the barkeep says, " That was the greatest song I've ever heard."

"Thanks. I wrote it myself."

"You ought to get a recording contract."

"I've tried, but no one will sign me," shrugged the piano player.

"They must be nuts," huffed the barkeep. "What do you call that song, anyways?"

"I Love You So Much I Could Shit."

Why did they fire the gay coach?
He had drilled everyone on the team.

"Mommy! Mommy! I don't
want to learn how to swim!"
"Shut up and get in the sack."

"Mommy! Mommy! I want to
play with grandpa!"
"Shut up and put the coffin lid
down!"

"Mommy! Mommy! Can I lick
the bowl?"
"Shut up and flush like
everyone else!"

Then there was the German lady who had quadruplets. She named them Adolph, Rudolph. Getoff and Stayoff.

A guy in a bar starts talking to a chick and asks, "What's your name?"

"Carmen," she replies. "It's not my real name, but the two things I like the most. Cars and men. What's your name?"

The guy thinks for a second. "Beerfuck."

A guy walks into a talent agents' office and says, "I've got a great act! You've never seen anything like it."

"And what would that be?" asks the skeptical agent.

"I sing through my butt!" announces the man proudly.

"Okay," nods the agent. "Show me."

So the guy drops his drawers and promptly starts to take a crap on the floor.

"Hey," cries the agent, "what the hell are you doing?"

"Clearing my throat."

Sex is like baseball.
The quality depends on who's
at bat.

A ninety two year old man
marries a sweet young thing of
20. On their wedding night he
climbs in bed with her and
holds up 4 fingers.
"Oh!" she exclaims. "Does this
mean we're going to do it 4
times?"
"No. It means "Take your
pick!"

It was an exciting day at the races and the clubhouse was filled with high rollers. One guy gets up ten minutes before the fourth race and bets $20,000 on number 2, much to the interest of the man at the next table.

Five minutes before post time the same man gets up and bets another $20,000 on number 2, again catching the eye of the man at the next table.

Two minutes to post time the high roller gets up again.

The observer says, "Excuse me, but you're not planning on betting number 2 again, are you?"

"Sure, he's a lock. Why?"

"Look, I own that horse. He has no speed, no endurance and is just out for exercise. He can't win."
"Maybe so, but I still think he'll win. You see, I own the other four horses."

What happened when the geek had his identity stolen?
The thief got so bored, he returned it.

Getting a blow job from an 80 year old is like tightrope walking. You don't want to look down.

Bill Gates and the president of GM were having lunch together.

"You know," observes Gates, "if you had kept up with technology like we have we'd have cars that cost $2000 and get 100 miles to the gallon."

"Maybe," replies the GM president, "but who wants a car that crashes three times a day?"

DIVERSITY
Hiring people who look different, but think like the boss.

The Secret Of Success
Work hard, stay focused and
marry a Kennedy

Why do farts smell?
So deaf people can enjoy them,
too.

"You and your suicide
attempts! Just look at the gas
bill!"

A father picks up the phone
and is greeted with this request:
"Dad, can I stay out 'til
eleven?"
"Sure."
"Thanks!" Click.
"Who was that?" called out his
wife from the kitchen.
"Just one of the boys asking to
stay out late."
"Not our boys. They're both
down in the basement."

If you don't know what you're
talking about, how do you
know when you're done?

The misunderstood teenager turned 18, stormed into the house, confronted his parents and ranted, "I'm outta here! I joined the Army!"
"The Army? Why?"
"I'm sick of taking orders."

"My husband's been caught screwing one of his patients and now it looks like he'll be fired!"
"That's terrible, but at least things couldn't get worse"
"Yes, they can. He's a veterinarian!"

A man and wife got into a heated argument and didn't speak to each other for three days. On the third day the man was looking through his closet and asked, "Do you know where my yellow shirt is.?"

"Oh, so now that you want something, you're speaking to me?"

Looking confused, the husband asked, "What are you talking about?"

"We haven't spoken for three days."

"Oh. I just thought we were getting along."

A guy is about to get married and his buddies are throwing a bachelor party. He gets picked up by one of his friends and on the way the friend just can't keep his mouth shut.

"This is going to be great! We're going to have booze and drugs and girls and porno flicks!"

"Aren't porno flicks a little dated?"

"Not when they star your fiancé."

Men want from their women the same thing they want from their underwear. A little bit of support and a little bit of freedom.

Two guys meet in a bar and start shooting the bull.

"Say," asks the first, "if you were at a party, got drunk, passed out and woke up with a condom in your ass, would you freak out?"

"Nah."

"Want to go to a party?"

My wife was after me to paint the shed for weeks, but I kept putting it off and she finally got so mad she painted it herself. I like women who get mad like that.

What do submariners call
battleships?
Targets.

A guy comes home and finds
his wife in bed with another
man.
"Hey," he shouts, "who said
you could fuck my wife?"
"Everybody."

"Marriage is toughest the first
ten years."
"How long have you been
married?"
'Ten years."

"Hey, buddy, your wife just fell in the well!"
"That's okay, we use city water now."

The Lone Ranger and Tonto found themselves surrounded by 10,000 Apaches on the warpath.
"Well," said the Lone Ranger, This looks like where we'll bite the dust."
"What do you mean "We," paleface?"

"How did you meet your wife?"
We were matched up by a computer dating service."
"That's it? That's the whole story?"
"Well they've fixed the computer since then."

"My wife and I have been married 25 years. If I'd have killed her when I first felt like it, I'd be out of jail by now."

How do you make a dog drink?
Put it in a blender.

A husband and wife were driving along and passed a billboard of a bikini clad beauty hawking beer.

"I suppose," mused the wife, "if I drank a six pack of that stuff, I'd look like her."

"No," said her husband, "if I drank a six pack of it, then you'd look like her."

What do you do with a dog that has no legs?
Take it for a drag.

A couple had just had their second child. For weeks prior the couple had been arguing about whether this would be their last, without settling the issue. The husband decided to ttake things into his own hands and while his wife was in the hospital had a vasectomy.

The next day he visited his wife and announced, "I won't be having any more kids. I've had a vasectomy."

"Well, I hope you'll love my next one like it's your own."

What has 8 teeth, 40 legs and smells like urine?
The front row of a Rolling Stones concert.

Civil engineers build targets. Mechanical engineers blow them up.

One thing women never say: "My, what an attractive scrotum!"

A waitress in a little restaurant notices 3 customers, all rednecks she'd never seen before, masturbating at their table.

"Hey, what do you think your doing?" she demanded.

"Well," gasped one, "the sign says "First come, First served.""

"Mommy, can I go swimming?"

"No, dear, the water's too deep."

"But Daddy's swimming!"

"Daddy's insured."

"I think my roommate is gay"
"Why do you say that?"
"His dick tastes like shit."

A stockbroker comes home early and finds his wife screwing another man.
"What the hell…?"
"Sorry, dear. I should have said something. I've gone public."

"Do these jeans make me look fat?"
"No, just fat enough."

Two Australians are stuck in a lifeboat together after their ship goes down. After a couple days a bottle bounces up against the boat. One of the Aussies opens it and out pops a genie.

"For rescuing me I'll grant you one wish," promises the genie. Without giving it any thought the first Aussie says, "Turn the ocean into Fosters!"

The genie nods his head, the ocean changes into beer and the genie disappears.

"Good work, knucklehead!" chides the second Aussie. "Now we'll have to pee in the boat!"

A wife was nagging her husband to get a hearing aid. "Look," she shouted, "they only cost about $3,000 dollars."
"Well, let me know when you say something worth $3,000, then I'll get one."

A little girl goes into a pet store and says sweetly to the owner, "I'd like to buy a bunny."
"That's nice," smiled the owner. "Would you like a white bunny or a black one?"
"I don't think my python cares."

A doctor, an accountant and a biker are all sitting at the counter at a truck stop and begin chatting.

"I bought my wife a diamond ring and a new car," brags the doctor. "I figured if she didn't like the ring, she'd like the car."

"I bought my wife a pendant and a speedboat," chimes in the accountant. "I figured if she didn't like the pendant, she'd love the speedboat."

"I got my bitch a t-shirt and a vibrator," said the biker. "I figured if she didn't like the t-shirt, she could go fuck herself."

What words do women hate to
hear most during sex?
"Hi, honey! I'm home!"

Have you noticed that if you
put the words "The" and "IRS
together it spells "Theirs?"

There's a new blonde paint on
the market.
It's cheap and it spreads easy.

A guy buys a camel from the zoo and begins riding it around town. He runs into a buddy of his.

"Hey, nice camel."

"Thanks."

"Is it a male or female?"

"Female."

"How can you tell?"

Everywhere I go people say "Look at the cunt on that camel!""

Willie split the baby's head
Wanted to see if brains are red
Mother, vexed, said to Father
"Raising boys is such a
          bother!"

A hunter got lost in the woods. He had a canteen of water, but after three days he was starving. Luckily, a bald eagle landed nearby and, with a fortunate throw, he killed the bird with a rock. He started a fire and proceeded to eat his catch. Just as he was finishing a park ranger found him and arrested him for killing a member of an endangered species.

In court the man explained the circumstances to the judge. "Well," said the judge, "all things considered, in this case I find you not guilty. But I'm curious. What does an eagle taste like?"

Well", replied the hunter, "it's sort of a cross between a whooping crane and a spotted owl."

A cop pulls over a woman driver who's weaving on the road. Smelling liquor on her breath, he makes her take a breathalyzer test.

"Well," he says, "it looks like you've had three or four stiff ones."

"Oh, my God! You mean it shows that too?"

"What seems to be the problem?" asked the psychiatrist.

"I don't have a problem. My family thinks I have a problem because I like cotton socks."

"Lots of people like cotton socks. Even I like cotton socks."

"Really? Do you prefer them with vinegar or just a squeeze of lemon?"

What do you call a musician who breaks up with his girlfriend?
Homeless.

A teen boy comes home and tells his biker dad, "Pop! I just got fucked for the first time!" "I'm proud of you, son," beamed the biker. "Now that you're a man, you can ride my hog!"
"I can't. My asshole hurts too much!"

My math instructor had a terrible car accident. He was grading papers on the curve.

"I only have two weeks to live? "I'll take the last week of July and the first week in August."

The Marines offer an early retirement bonus to soldiers with 10 or more years of service. The soldier gets to have the distance between any two body parts measured and gets a discharge bonus of $1,000 dollars an inch.

On one Texas base three vets sign up and meet the doctor for an official measurement.

The first guy wants measured from hand tip to hand tip.

"Six feet," confirms the doctor. "You get $72,000 dollars."

The second wants measured from the top of his head to his toes.

"Six feet, two inches," says the doc. "You get "74,000."

The third guy says "I want measured from the tip of my cock to the back of balls."
"Suit yourself, soldier," shrugs the doc. "Drop 'em!"
The Marine drops trow and the doctor goes to his knees to measure, stretches out the man's cock, and then nothing! "Hey!" exclaims the doc. "Where're your balls?:
"Baghdad."

"Grandmother! Use the bottle opener! You'll ruin your gums!"

The traffic cop pulled over a guy for speeding and asked to see his license and registration. "Sorry, I lost my license after my fifth DWI," explained the driver with a drunken slur, "but I have the registration in the glove compartment with my gun."

"Gun?" asked the cop.

"Yeah. I keep a gun in case anyone tries to hijack the drugs in the trunk."

Having heard enough the cop goes back to the car and calls the SWAT team. They arrive and search the car thoroughly, finding nothing. The SWAT captain approaches the driver and says, "There's no gun or drugs in your car."

"No kidding," said the driver soberly. "And I suppose that other cop told you I was drunk and speeding, too?"

Some new cons were in the prison yard talking.
"I'm in for armed robbery."
"I'm in for murder."
"I'm in for fucking dogs."
"Fucking dogs? How low can you get?"
"Well. I did a dachshund once."

A man and his wife were in the drugstore picking up a few things when the man remembered they were out of condoms. So they went to see the druggist.

"We have a new brand in," said the druggist. "Olympic condoms. They come in three colors: gold, silver and bronze."

"Get silver, dear," suggested the wife. "It would be nice if you came in second for a change."

What part of a woman does a man like looking at best?
The top of her head.

"How come your dad is so mad we borrowed his car last night?"
"That was him we ran down."

"My Mommy went to get Daddy a revolver for his birthday."
"Boy! I'll bet he'll be surprised!"
"Yeah. He doesn't even know she wants to shoot him."

"You must stop masturbating so frequently," said the optometrist.

"Why? Is it affecting my vision?"

"No, but it bothers my other patients in the waiting room."

A man nudges his wife at three a.m.

"Hey, honey, any chance for a blowjob?"

Groggy, she says. "Not now. Why don't you jerk off in a glass and I'll drink it in the morning."

A minister died and went to his eternal reward. He was disappointed when St. Peter showed him to a lowly shack. The next day he noticed a member of his congregation, a taxi driver, entering Heaven. St Peter showed him to a lovely estate.

"Hey, how come I get a shack and he gets a mansion?" asked the minister.

"When you preached, people slept. When he drove, people prayed."

"Are you scared of flying?"
"No, it's the crashing that bothers me."

Sheep are better than women. They don't care if you screw their sister.

Two women are in the supermarket together and come to the cantaloupes.
"Wow, these remind me of my husbands' balls!" exclaims the first.
"That big?"
"That dirty."

"You must be the worst lover I ever had!"
"How could you know that in just 10 seconds."

"Knock! Knock!"
"Who's there?"
"Control freak! Now you say
"Control freak who?""

A guy walks into a bar and
sees a beautiful babe sitting by
herself. He walks over and
says, "Hi, babe! Would you
like a little company?"
"Why, do you have one to
sell?"

Don't be sexist.
Broads hate that.

Two attorneys walk into a restaurant and order coffee. The waitress brings over the drinks and the attorneys each pull a sandwich out of their briefcases and begin unwrapping them.

"Hey," says the waitress, "you can't eat your own food in here!"

The attorneys look at each other, shrug and trade sandwiches.

"I was an earth sign. He was a water sign. Together, we made mud."

A salesman knocks on the door of a nice house. He's shocked when a boy no older than nine or ten opens the door with a cigarette hanging out of his mouth and an open beer can in his hand.

"Is you're mother home?"

"What do you think?"

Why does sex bring a tear to Mike Tyson's eye?

Mace.

A soldier is home on leave and visiting his girl.

"So there we were in our parachutes 10,000 feet in the air and I was afraid to jump. The sergeant said, "If you don't jump I'm going to stick my dick up your ass.""

"So did you jump?"

"Just a little. At first."

What do a vagina and a warm toilet seat have in common? They're both nice, but you wonder where they've been.

Scientists perfected a new and ethical cloning technique and decided everyone should have a copy of themselves stored away until they died. At first they were going to go in alphabetical order, but many people without relatives argued that they should be first so if something happened to them they could carry on the family name.

This sounded reasonable to the scientist and so they decreed, "Let he who is without kin stash the first clone!"

The teacher is addressing her class the day before the big test. "There's no excuse for being absent tomorrow except a death in the family or medical emergency."

A smartass in the back calls out, "What if I show up with sexual exhaustion?"

"Then you can write with your other hand."

A woman who was running late dashed toward church. As she approached the church she asked a passerby, "Is Mass out?"

"No, but your hat's on crooked."

The doctor, reviewing the test results, turned to his patient and said, "You've got ten."
"Ten what?" demanded the patient. "Ten weeks? Ten months?"
"Nine…."

A young man graduates college and grabs a cab to go to the airport for the trip home. "I just graduated Harvard and I just can't wait to get out and see the world.
"Congratulations!" offered the cabbie, extending his hand. "I'm Justin, Class of '60."

A guy appears before St Peter, seeking admittance through the pearly gates.

"Can you tell me one good deed you did?" asked Peter.

"I stopped some gangstas from harassing an old lady."

"When did you do that?"

"About two minutes ago."

A man gets some groceries and is in the checkout line.

"You must be single," says the clerk.

"You can tell that from my groceries?"

"No, because you're ugly."

A redneck comes home for dinner and is shocked when his wife puts a plate of grass on the table.
"Hey, what the hell is this?
"I figured if it's good enough for your girlfriend, it's good enough for you."

A philosopher is a person who doesn't have a job, but understands why.

Therapy is expensive
Popping bubble wrap is cheap.
You choose.

A guy rushes into a proctologists' office and says, "You got to help me, Doc! I'm constipated and it feels like something's stuck up my butt!"

So the doctor examines him and says, "There is something in here." He reaches in and pulls out a one hundred dollar bill. "Money!" says the doctor,. "You've got money stuck up your butt. I think there's more!" So he pulls out bill after bill. Finally, he sighs, "That's the last of it."

"How much is there?"

"$1999.

"I knew I wasn't feeling too grand!"

A man is sitting in the movie theater. A few minutes before the film is to start a bear comes in and sits in front of him. Startled, the man asks, "Are you a bear?"

"As a matter of fact, I am."

"What are you doing coming to a movie?"

"Well, I liked the book."

Willie, hitting at a ball,
Drove a liner down the hall.
Through the door came Dr.
      Hill.
Several teeth are missing still.

Why did the Pope cross the road?
He crosses everything.

How many lawyer jokes are there?
Three. The rest are all true stories.

A gay guy goes into a deli and asks for a salami.
"Would you like that sliced?" asks the counterman.
"Do I look like a slot machine?"

Mary had a little lamb
Before she learned to think
Now she's blond
And men are fond
Of keeping her in mink

I have my standards.
They're low, but I have them.

Your problem is low self
esteem. It's very common
among losers.

"Young man, where do you work?" the judge asked the defendant.

"Here and there."

"What do you do?"

"This and that."

"That's enough crap," said the judge, "lock him up."

"Hey, when will I get out?"

"Sooner or later."

Then there were the gay outlaws. They rode into town and shot up the sheriff.

Why did God invent yeast
infections?
So women could learn what
it's like to live with an
irritating cunt.

What do a blonde and a turtle
have in common?
Get them on their backs and
they're both fucked.

Early to bed, early to rise
And your girl goes out
With other guys.

Senator Obama is touring a health care facility with the Chief of Medicine. As they pass a room they see a man masturbating into a bottle.

"What's going on here, asks Obama.

"That man has a medical condition that causes his testicles to fill up rapidly," explains the doctor. "He must relieve himself five times a day."

They move on and come to a man getting a blowjob from a nurse.

"And what is this?"

"Same condition. Better health care plan."

Two families move to the U.S. from Pakistan. Before they go their separate ways the fathers make a bet over which will be more American in one year, A year later they get together. The first man says, "I am a real American! My son is quarterback of the football team, I eat breakfast at McDonald's every morning and I'm on my way to the ballpark to root for my team." The second man say, "Fuck, you, towel-head."

Little Willie gets up to go the bathroom in the middle of the night, passes his parents room and sees them fucking.

The next morning he asks his mother, "Why were you doing what you were doing last night?"

I was doing that because I want a little baby," she explains.

The next night Willie gets up again and this night sees mom giving dad a blowjob.

The next morning he asks mom, "Were you doing that because you want a baby?"

"No, dear. Mommy was doing that because she wants a BMW."

What has four legs and bleeds easily?
Half a dog.

If God is watching us the least you could do is be entertaining.

I used to be into necrophilia, sadomasochism, and bestiality, but my therapist told me I was beating a dead horse.

A wife is angry because her husband is out drinking every night. So one night she storms out of the house and down to the bar. There's her husband at a table, a glass of something in front of him, yukking it up with some buddies.
She marches to the table, plops herself down and says,
"Two can play this game!"
With that she grabs his glass and gulps it down. Then she spits it out in disgusted. "That stuff's horrible!" she exclaims.
"There, you see," said her husband. "And you thought I've been enjoying myself!"

How many sex therapists does it take to screw in a light bulb? Two. One to screw it in and one to tell him he's doing it wrong.

String Theory is like a penis. The more you think about it, the harder it gets.

I used to have a drug problem, but then I won some money.

Have you seen the new French
army flag?
It's a white cross on a white
background.

A guy is sitting next to an old
drunk at the bar when he
notices an awful odor.
"Christ," says the guy to the
old man, "did you shit your
pants?"
"Yep."
"Why didn't you go to the
john?"
"I ain't done yet."

How many men do you need
for a Mafia funeral?
Just one. To slam down the
trunk.

Date the homeless. You can
drop them off anywhere.

Smoking is a leading cause of
statistics.

A man goes to visit his friend, an Irishman. He knocks on the door and his Irish friend lets him in.

"Good to see ya," says the Irishman. "Perhaps you can help me with a problem I'm having?"

"Sure."

So the Irishman shows his friend to the kitchen and points to the table.

"I can't seem to get this jigsaw puzzle."

"Put the cornflakes back in the box."

What do you call 20 politicians skydiving?
Air pollution.

What did the hillbilly girl say when she lost her virginity?
"Get offa me, Daddy! You're crushin' my cigarettes."

Build a man a fire and he'll be warm for a day.
Set a man on fire and he'll be warm the rest of his life.

A guy walks into a bar with a cork stuck up his butt.
"What happened to you?" asked the barkeep.
"I freed a genie from a bottle. He said he'd give me one wish and I said "No shit!""

First taxes and death were inevitable, Now there's shipping and handling.

How many congressmen does it take to take down a picture? Ten. One to hold the picture and nine to tear down the wall.

How do you get a woman off during sex?
Push her.

Work off excess weight.
Steal something heavy.

Why are hangovers better than women?
Hangovers go away.

A vampire walks into a blood bank.
"Two pints to go, please."

What's the worst thing about unemployment?
It's harder to fuck your girlfriend when her husband's home.

The following sentence is true.
The previous sentence is false.

What's worse than a dog licking your butt during sex? Liking it.

What do you do if a pit bull humps your leg? You let him.

What's the last thing a redneck stripper takes off? Her bowling shoes.

"Could you suggest a birthday present for my aunt? She's eighty and very wealthy."
"How about some floor wax?"

"I lost my legs in a railroad accident."
"Did the railroad treat you right?"
"I can't kick."

LAWYER
A man who makes sure he gets what's coming to you.

Willie scalped his baby brother
Left him lying hairless.
"Willie," said his worried Ma,
"Try not to be so careless."

If a slice of bread always lands
butter side down, if you butter
both sides, will it float forever?

First kid: "I have a problem. I
have a crush on my teacher."
Second kid: "So what?
Everybody gets a crush on
their teacher."
First kid: "Yeah, but I'm home
schooled."

A guy goes into the hospital for a vasectomy. When he wakes up the doctor is by his bed.

"I'm sorry," says the doc, "but we screwed up and took off your penis by mistake. So we went ahead and did a complete sex change operation instead."

"Oh, my God!" exclaimed the man. "I'll never have another erection!"

"Sure you will. It just won't be yours."

What's the matter with you?"
screamed the pedestrian. "Are
you blind?"
"Blind? I hit ya, didn't I?"

"Can Willie come out and
play?"
"Don't be silly. You know he
has no arms or legs."
"Yeah, we need him for
second base."

"Here's your cigar back. I
heard your baby died."

"Mommy! Mommy! What's for dinner?"
"Shut up and get back in the oven."

"Mommy! Mommy! Can we have Granny for dinner?"
"No! We still have half of Aunt Sophie in the freezer."

"Mommy! Mommy! Can I play the piano?"
"No. your hooks would scratch the keys."

Why does Washington have the U.S. Congress and New Jersey toxic waste dumps? New Jersey had first choice.

A newsboy is going down the street hawking papers.
"Two hundred twelve people taken in porno scam!"
"Here, boy," said a business man, handing the boy fifty cents. "I'll take one."
"Thanks, mister!" The boy then continued down the street..
"Two hundred thirteen people taken in porno scam!"

I love being married. It's so gratifying finding that one special person you want to annoy the rest of your life.

"I'm trying a new course to improve my memory."
"How does it work?"
"I lend money."

Two old ladies were talking.
"Do you have mutual orgasm?"
"I think we have State Farm."

For a lark a guy visiting an amusement park stops in to see the fortune teller.
"A long forgotten loved one will soon appear," says the gypsy woman. "Buy the negatives at any price."

I'd like to give you the gift you need, but I don't know how to wrap a bathtub.

Never pick up a woman at a laundromat.
If she can't afford a washing machine then how can she keep you in beer?

Men are like wine.
They start out green like
grapes, women stomp on them,
keep them in the dark, and let
them age until they are
something fit to have dinner
with.

A blonde is on the subway,
reading a newspaper. A
headline blared, "12 Brazilian
Soldiers Killed"
She turned to the man next to
her and asked, "How many is a
Brazilian?"

Eat Right
Exercise
Die Anyway

Cat
The other white meat.

I like cats. Let's trade recipes!

The Addams Children's Library

Dad's New Wife Robert
Fun Four Letter Words
Kid's Guide To Hitchhiking
The Sissy Who Snitched
Grandpa Gets A Casket
Human Anatomy Pop-Ups
Some Kittens Can Fly
What Those Dogs Are Doing
Mickey Meets The
    Taxidermist
Strangers Have Great Candy
You're Different. That's Bad
Nightmares Are Real
Exploring Inside Refrigerators
Mr. Fork Meets Mr. Outlet
Eggs, Toilet Paper and School
Playgrounds: Respect Through
    Fear

Be Naughty
Save Santa The Trip

Cannibals won't eat clowns.
They taste funny.

Celebrate Thanksgiving the old
fashioned way. Invite the
neighbors over, eat turkey, kill
them and take their land.

A farmer is walking through a wooded section of his property when he hears some splashing from his pond. He goes over to investigate and finds three young women skinny dipping. "Howdy!" he calls out.

The women squeal and make for the far end of the pond. "We're not getting out 'til you go away!" yells one.

"That's okay, I won't be long," assures the farmer. "I just came by to feed the alligator."

How can you spot Ronald McDonald at a nudist colony? Sesame seed buns.

A redneck and his wife were sitting on the porch in the early evening.

"Next week is our fiftieth anniversary, Ma," drawls the husband.

"We could have a party," suggested Ma. "We could kill the pig."

"Why blame the pig for something that happened fifty years ago?"

What's the difference between boogers and broccoli?
Kids don't eat broccoli.

Date A Butcher
Play for bigger steaks

What's white on the outside
and green on the inside?
A frog sandwich.

Little Willie was chemist
Little Willie is no more
For what he thought was H_2O
Was H_2SO_4.

A boy comes in from a day at play. He has a chair under each arm and a sofa strapped to his back.

"Where did you get that?" asked his dad.

"From a guy in the park."

The dad then belted his son.

"What have I told you about taking suites from strangers?"

If at first you don't succeed, reload.

When buying a lawnmower select one sure to last your wife several years.

Be A Winner!
Pick a fight with a 4 year old

How many male chauvinists does it take to change a light bulb?
None. She can cook in the dark.

An astronaut back from the
    Stars
Was bragging in all of the bars
"You see, this here penis
Won prizes on Venus
And took second place up on
    Mars."

It's better to be wanted for
murder than not wanted at all.

I like being eighty. It's harder
for the sexual harassment
charges to stick.

What do they call "Star Trek" in Japan?
"Sulu, Master Navigator"

A man is driving through the city when his car breaks down. He gets out and starts fiddling under the hood. Then he hears noise from the back of the car. He checks and finds a punk trying to break into the trunk. "Hey, this is my car!"
"Okay, you take the front. I'll take the rear."

Traffic is jammed up on the Washington street. A cop is going from car to car, talking to the drivers.

"What's going on?" asks a driver.

"Congress is refusing to pass George Bush's Iraqi spending bill. He's holed up in the White House and threatening to douse himself with gasoline and light up if the money isn't forthcoming. So we're taking a collection."

"How much have you got so far?"

"33 gallons."

I need someone really bad.
Are you really bad?

A man gets a $100 fine for
speeding. As he pays the clerk
of courts gives him a receipt.
"What the hell am I supposed
to do with this?"
"Keep it," says the clerk.
"Collect three and you get a
bicycle."

Going to comedian school was
easy. All the classes were a
joke.

Look for all these Politicsisfun.com books
coming soon:

Politically Incorrect Blond, Brunette And Redhead
        Jokes.
Little Willie's Rhymes and Crimes
Autistic Loves: Vignettes Of Joy
2008 T-Shirt Wit And Wisdom
Success Secrets Of The Illuminati
Politically Incorrect Female Chauvinist Jokes
        About Men

All will be exclusively available through
Amazon.com

Search on the author's name, James Buffington, for
these and future titles.

Jim has been collecting jokes and humor for over thirty years. Having graduated Cleveland State in 1974, he spent the next 23 years in a variety of positions while pursuing the lifestyle of a bridge bum. Currently Jim operates the popular gift and t-shirt site, politicsisfun.com. He was finally corralled by his wife, Gail, in 1997. They have 3 children, 2 of which are autistic. Proceeds from this book and other endeavors are for their future. They currently reside in Northeast Ohio. The family is owned by 2 cats, Callie and The Gray, who attend to all their spiritual needs.

Jim is available for hire for humor and writing projects and may be reached at jimbuf2000@gmail.com

CPSIA information can be obtained at www.ICGtesting.com
Printed in the USA
LVOW111745160512

282041LV00018B/111/P

9 781440 402401